Jes(
Our Light

'The Lord is with you and has greatly blessed you'
Luke 1: 28

The Benedictine Nuns
of Turvey Abbey

Additional material by Mark Poulter

McCrimmons
Great Wakering Essex England

First published in 2000 by
McCRIMMON PUBLISHING CO LTD
10-12 High Street, Great Wakering, Essex SS3 0EQ
Telephone: 01702 218956
Fax: 01702 216082
Email: mccrimmons@dial.pipex.com
Web site: www.mccrimmons.co.uk

Jesus, Our Light   ISBN 0 85597 611 X

Jesus, Our Hope   ISBN 0 85597 612 8
Jesus, Our Way   ISBN 0 85597 613 6

Edited and additional information by Mark Poulter
All images are taken from original paintings by the Benedictine
Nuns of Turvey Abbey, part of the *Jesus, Our Life series of posters.*
Typeset in Frutiger Light 11.5/13.5pt, 10/12pt and ITC Fenice
Regular Italic 24/26pt
Printed by Thanet Press Ltd., Margate, Kent

Contents

Jesus, Our Light
The early life of Jesus

Introduction

The stunning set of 11 posters which accompany this book follows the early part of Jesus's life, from the Annunciation, through his birth in Bethlehem to his childhood, and eventually to the beginning of the Ministry of Our Lord when Jesus calls the first disciples. The dominating theme of this is Christ as the source of Light and Life. It is shown in the pictures as light shining on and through people and things.

Using this booklet

This booklet is designed to help teachers, catechists, R.E. co-ordinators and others to make the most of these beautiful images. On each page the artist has sought to describe her inspiration for each painting by reflecting on the relevant scripture references. We have also included:

- a picture of the poster;

- a quote from scripture; and,

- questions for discussion.

Page 31 of this book includes a cross-reference to themes and topics, such as those included in popular education programmes like *Here I Am* and *Walk With Me*. You may also wish to use some of the ideas that follow.

Discussion and teaching

The Questions for Discussion included in this booklet are designed to help teachers and catechists develop the responses of children to these well-known Bible stories. If you have time, we suggest you look up the scriptural reference yourself and reflect on it. Why not use a piece of the text as a heading for a display or a starting point for a session? And if you are stuck for time, you may want to use the scriptural quote we have selected. We do not aim to offer formulaic lessons and hope you will adapt and alter the material to suit the needs of the children in your care.

Display and decoration

The vibrant and striking colours of the paintings means they are ideally suited to display in Church, on notice-boards, as the centre piece of an R.E. display or prayer table/altar, or around school. You may wish to copy or type out one or more of the Questions for Discussion on each page and arrange them with the poster/s to make your displays more interactive and appealing to children and adults alike.

Assemblies and services

The posters are deal for use in assemblies and services. You may want to display them as a basis for discussion or as a stimulus for prayer or reflection. They will also add colour and meaning to Bible stories read or acted out in the parish or school.

Prayer and meditation

A striking visual image often helps people to pray, meditate or reflect. You could use one or more of the posters as a focal point for an altar/prayer table or as the centre piece of a prayer service. This book and it's associated set of posters is particularly suited to themes such as Light, Life and the power of God. As many of the stories cover Advent and Christmas, these images are appropriate to many of the Autumn topics of popular R.E. programmes, such as Birthdays, Preparations, Gifts and Visitors. (Please see page 31 for more themes.)

Creative writing and artwork

The rich and vivid colour of these illustrations, combined with the powerful imagery, makes them an ideal starting point for creative work. Why not use them to provoke thought and discussion before writing poetry or prayers? Or how about asking children to copy or re-design an image as part of their art work?

And finally...

Why not share your ideas and experiences with us?

We are always interested in finding out what works well and what materials you need to better fulfil your ministry.

Contact us at:
MCCRIMMONS, Freepost CL2425,
Southend-on-Sea, Essex, SS3 0BR.
01702-218956 (phone)   01702-216082 (fax)
mccrimmons@dial.pipex.com (email)
www.mccrimmons.co.uk (Web site)

Close your eyes and imagine you are walking in the busy city of Nazareth. You stop outside a small, rather poor looking house. Sit down and rest awhile.

There's a young girl sweeping her small room. She is singing as she works. Listen – she is singing about her God who is mighty and powerful. Every so often she stops and rests on her broom. Watch as she gazes out of her window. What is she thinking about?

All of a sudden the room is filled with a very bright light. The young girl shields her eyes and kneels down on the floor. Watch her face. She seems to be talking to someone. Perhaps she is afraid? You are as still as she is.

Then you hear a voice saying, *"Mary, do not be afraid."* She really does look frightened. Listen to the voice again. What does it all mean?

"You are going to have a child and he will be called Jesus. He will be great and will be called the son of the Most High."

Watch as Mary begins to smile. Her voice is loud and clear as she says, *"Behold the handmaid of the Lord; let what you have said be done to me."*

The bright light is starting to fade. Mary looks calm. She is sitting in the middle of the room thinking. What will she tell Joseph?

1 Annunciation

Luke 1: 26-38

The light is in the centre of the painting, where the Holy Spirit overshadows Mary with God's Light. Both Mary and the Angel derive light from that Light, the light breaking up in colours, supplanting the receding darkness. The power and strength of the Light remind us there is nothing that God cannot do.

'The Lord is with you and has greatly blessed you.'

Luke 1: 28

Questions for discussion

What things are you afraid of?

Who helps you when you are worried or frightened?

Is it sometimes difficult to do the things you know are right?

What is God asking you to do?

How can you ask God for help with the things you find difficult?

What will you do to answer God's call?

Mary is getting herself ready for a very long journey. She is going to visit her cousin Elizabeth. Watch as she packs together all the things she thinks she will need. Mary has been thinking about her cousin. She knows deep in her heart that it is very important to see her as soon as possible.

Mary is travelling with a group of people. Watch as the group journeys through day and night. It is a hard trip. Sometimes the donkeys really struggle to climb up steep hills.

Mary is ready to say goodbye to the group now she is getting closer to Zechariah's house. Zechariah is Elizabeth's husband. Mary picks up her small bundles and hurries towards the house. It's evening now and the bright light of a lamp looks very welcoming.

Watch as Elizabeth runs out to meet her. Mary and Elizabeth hold each other tightly. Their faces both look tired but very happy.

Elizabeth is an old lady but as she listens to Mary she begins to feel full of energy. Listen as she begins to speak. She has a message from God. *"Blessed are you among women, and blessed is the fruit of your womb."*

Watch as Mary closes her eyes and remembers when God gave her a message that she was going to have a very special baby. Elizabeth is going to give birth to a special child too.

Mary and Elizabeth are still holding each other. Mary begins to praise God for the wonderful things God has done. Are there things for which you would like to praise God?

2 Visitation

Luke 1: 39-56

The light is in the hearts of Mary and Elizabeth, in their wombs where Jesus and John meet. The light around Mary and Elizabeth in the painting suggests the still hidden Dawn, driving the shades away.

'Mary said, My heart praises the Lord;'

Luke 1: 46

Questions for discussion

Who do you share good news with?

Do you tell your family or one of your friends?

What do your friends say when you give them good news?

What wonderful things has God done for you?

Can you think of ways that you can praise God?

There has been great rejoicing in your village. Everybody has been talking about how wonderful God is and how he always keeps his promises. God promised that Elizabeth would have a baby. Elizabeth is old – everybody thought she was too old to have a baby.

The baby is eight days old now. He is lying in his mother's arms. Watch them for a moment.

It's time to choose a name for the baby. Listen to all of Elizabeth's neighbours and relations chattering and discussing which name he should have. Everybody thinks it should be Zechariah, like his father. What do you think it should be?

Look at Elizabeth's face. She doesn't agree. She is smiling a warm, wise smile.
She says his name is to be John.

The neighbours and relations look very puzzled. They have gone to find Zechariah. But Zechariah can't speak. He's old and slow. His face lights up when he looks at his son in Elizabeth's arms.

Watch as he reaches for his writing tablet and slowly writes, "His name is John". Everyone is amazed. They know this is the work of God, a God who keeps promises.

"His name is John," says Zechariah. Everyone turns to look at him. It's a miracle – he can speak again.

Listen as the people begin to praise God for keeping the promise to Elizabeth and Zechariah. How do you know God keeps promises made to you?

3 Birth of John the Baptist

Luke 1: 57-80

Here the light of the rising sun has gained in strength. The time is nearer and yet still hidden. John seems to be saying, "I am not the Light, I am only heralding the Light that comes after me." John points with his hand to the rising son as his father praises God.

'He has come to the help of his people and has set them free.'

Luke 1: 68

Questions for Discussion

Why were Elizabeth and Zechariah so happy?

How did God keep a promise to them?

When did you join God's family? What promises did you make?

What would you like to thank God for?

How can you thank God for everything you have been given?

What promises can you make to God now?

Imagine you are on a long journey. You have been travelling for days and are all going to the same place – Bethlehem. The Emperor, Caesar Augustus has told everybody to enrol so he can be sure all the taxes are paid.

You've become friendly with a kind young man and a beautiful young woman called Joseph and Mary. Sometimes Joseph lets you lead the donkey that Mary is sitting on. Mary is going to have a baby very soon. She looks tired but happy. Joseph sometimes looks worried. Watch his face as he checks that Mary has enough blankets wrapped around her.

You can see the bright lights of Bethlehem at last. It is very busy. There are people everywhere laughing and shouting. This would be a frightening place to get lost!

You've been so busy looking at the crowded streets and haven't noticed that Mary is holding Joseph's hand very tightly. Watch as Joseph helps her down from the donkey. They must find somewhere to stay.

Joseph takes Mary from one inn to another. But everywhere is full. Joseph decides to try one last place. There's a lot of noise coming from the inn. Surely there won't be room here?

Watch as the innkeeper points to the back of the inn. He's pointing to the stable. Walk with Mary and Joseph and take a look inside. It's warm and a little dark.
The cattle are lying on the straw. It's not much but Mary and Joseph are just pleased to have found somewhere.

You go to the innkeeper to ask for a spare lamp. When you come back a baby is crying. Mary has had her baby. She smiles at you and calls you over to the manger. What can you see? What will you say to Mary, Joseph and Jesus?

4 *Nativity* Part 1 – The Birth of Jesus

Luke 2: 1-7

The Light radiates out in clear circles into the darkness of the cave and into the night from which the shepherds emerge. The animals too are caught up in the Light!

'She gave birth to her first son, wrapped him in strips of cloth and laid him in a manger.'

Luke 2: 7

Questions for discussion

Do you think Joseph and Mary were pleased to go on a long journey?

How do you think they felt when they arrived in Bethlehem?

Have you ever been to any strange places?
How did they make you feel?

Imagine you were with Mary and Joseph.
How would you explain what happened?

You are the first person to see the baby Jesus.
What would you tell him?

Imagine you are sitting on a hillside in Bethlehem. You are warming your hands around your lamp and staring out into the night. You are a shepherd and night after night you watch the sunset and lead your sheep into safe pastures.

Tonight you have been sitting with the other shepherds watching the stars.

There's one star shining brighter than all the others. As you watch the star, you listen to the others talking. They have heard people in the town saying that a special baby is going to be born. A special baby who is going to save his people. How can a baby do that you wonder?

Your friends have stopped talking and you can hear a strange noise. Listen, it's the sound of singing... joyful singing!

The sky is suddenly filled with bright light. It's so bright you can hardly see.

You fall to the ground and your heart is beating very fast. You hear a voice saying, *"Do not be afraid. Look, I bring you news of great joy, a joy to be shared by all the people. Today, in the town of David, a saviour has been born to you. He is Christ the Lord."*

The voice tells you to go and find a baby lying in a manger. You are shocked but the other shepherds are picking up their crooks and running, running as fast as they can. You try to keep up with them. Look up into the sky and see the bright star guiding you.

You have reached the manger. You've brought your best crook as a present for this special baby. Watch the faces of Joseph and Mary as you lay your crook in front of Jesus. Stop and think. What would you most like to give Jesus?

4 *Nativity* Part 2 – The Shepherds

Luke 2: 8-20

The Light radiates out in clear circles into the darkness of the cave and into the night from which the shepherds emerge.

The animals too are caught up in the Light!

'Glory to God in the highest heaven.'

Luke 2: 14

Questions for discussion

How do you think the shepherds felt when the angels appeared?

What things make you afraid?

How can you share the joy of Christmas with your friends and family?

What present can you give to Jesus?

How can you serve Jesus during your life?

Imagine you are sitting just inside the temple at Jerusalem. It's very hot today. You are glad to be out of the sun and are leaning against a large, cool pillar.

It's dark inside the temple. There's just enough light for you to be able to see a very old woman. She's been here all day praying. Watch as she leads her husband Simeon. He is blind and moves very slowly.

Simeon and Anna have found themselves a place to sit. Look at them. They look as if they are waiting for something or somebody. Now you can hear the sound of a small baby crying. Mary, Joseph and Jesus are making their way towards Simeon and Anna.

Watch as Simeon takes Jesus in his arms. Simeon can't see the face of Jesus clearly. Watch as his old hand gently touches the face he can't see. Simeon knows that this is his Saviour.

Now Anna takes the baby in her arms. She is smiling. This is the child she has longed to hold.

Now it's your turn. Take Jesus in your arms. Spend a few moments looking at his face. What do you see?

Now give the baby back to Mary. Tell her what you saw.

5 Presentation

Luke 2: 22-38

Jesus is the strong centre of the light, as the theme of light dominates in the liturgy of this feast. The light's effects are far-reaching. Jesus is not only the Light of all Israel but also of the gentiles and everyone else across the world.

'Simeon took the child in his arms and gave thanks to God.'

Luke 2: 28

Questions for discussion

Have you ever really wanted something? What was it?

How do you feel when you have to wait and can't have something straight away?

Imagine you are looking forward to a special day.
How does it feel when the day finally arrives?

How can you thank God for all the special times you have been given?

You've been travelling for days, travelling from the East. It's your job to make sure that your master's camels get enough food and rest. Your master has been following a bright star. He has told you it will lead him to a very special baby. Look up at the star. Will it really lead you to a baby?

You've settled for the night and, as you prepare the fire, you listen to your master and his friends talking. They've been studying the stars and the Bible for years. They are certain that this bright star will lead them to a Saviour – a Saviour for the whole world.

All of a sudden their talking stops. The star has stopped. It has come to rest, showing the very place where the baby was born.

Gather your things together and hurry with your master and his friends. The star is getting brighter and brighter. You've come to a stable. Can this be the place?

Watch as your master falls to his knees and brings out of his cloak a box of shining gold. Your master's friends fall to their knees too and carefully bring gifts of frankincense and myrrh.

Look at Mary and Joseph. They are smiling because they know their baby is very special. You don't have anything so precious to give to Jesus. Instead, tell Mary that you know their baby is special.

It's time to go now. Watch as your master and his friends bow very deeply to Jesus. Wait for them to leave the stable. It's just you and Jesus. Worship him now in your own way.

6 The Magi

Matthew 2: 1-12

Simeon's prophecy is already fulfilled: the Light has reached out to the Pagan world. The picture's source of light is the star but the Magi are concentrating on something else. Their attention is with the Light the star has led them to.

'We saw his star when it came up in the east, and we have come to worship him.'

Matthew 2: 2

Questions for discussion

How do you feel at the end of a long journey?

Are you tired or excited?

What did the Magi give to Jesus?

What presents can you give to Jesus today?

How do you know that Jesus is your special friend?

How many different ways can you think to worship Jesus?

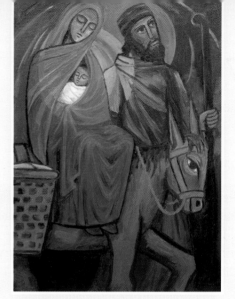

Imagine that you are Joseph. It's late at night and you find that you can't sleep. You get up. Now turn and watch Mary and Jesus sleeping peacefully together. The sky is filled with stars. Look out into the night. Something has disturbed your peace. You feel troubled but don't know what it is.

Go back to bed. You fall asleep and dream that an angel comes to you with a message. The angel gives you a warning that Herod wants to kills Jesus. You must hurry to Egypt.

Mary has woken up and you tell her your news. Watch her face as she realises her baby is in danger.

Mary wraps Jesus in blankets. Go and untie the donkey. Quickly. It's going to be a long journey to Egypt.

It's early morning and the sun is rising, filling the sky with colours of purple, red and pink. Your heart is beating faster. You know you must be quick to avoid danger, to escape from Herod. Listen as Mary sings gently to Jesus. Jesus looks safe and warm. Does he know he is in danger?

As the sun sets you are still travelling. The road is long and hard but you must now stop. Still Mary sings. She sings of God and his great power. God will protect us, God is our safety.

You reach Egypt at last. Mary and Jesus are safe. God has protected you.

Leave Mary and Joseph now. How does God keep you safe?

7 Flight into Egypt

Matthew 2: 13-15

Darkness seems overwhelming here, in complete contrast to the light of the preceding pictures. But despite the gloom, the darkness cannot kill the Light hidden under Mary's cloak. Joseph is looking up in absolute trust: his faith is not shaken by the darkness.

'Get up, take the child and his mother and escape to Egypt.'

Matthew 2: 13

Questions for discussion

Have you ever been in danger? What happened?

What makes you really scared?

Who looks after you when you are frightened?

How does it feel when someone comforts and protects you?

How does God keep you safe?

How can you tell God you need help? What will you ask?

Imagine you are travelling with a large group of relatives and friends. You've been to Jerusalem to celebrate a very big feast. It was the feast of the Passover. You've made friends with a boy called Jesus. He is twelve years old – just like you. Jesus is always reading and studying. He has been helping you.

Mary, Jesus' mother, comes to ask you if you have seen Jesus. She looks worried. She hasn't seen her son since they left Jerusalem. Watch as Mary goes to look for Joseph. Joseph looks anxious too. He hasn't seen Jesus either.

Mary and Joseph will have to go back to Jerusalem. The sun is setting and the sky is filled with colours of red and orange. Follow Mary and Joseph as they head for the bright lights of the city of Jerusalem. Listen to them as they walk along. They are really worried. Jesus has never done anything like this before.

As you get nearer to the temple you can hear a voice that you recognise. It's your friend Jesus. He is sitting with a group of the teachers of the Law. They are all listening to him.

Mary and Joseph are amazed. Their faces look puzzled now, not anxious. Watch as Jesus leaves the teachers and greet his parents. What are they saying?

Jesus smiles and says, "Why were you looking for me? Did you not know I must be in my Father's house?"

Joseph puts his arm around Jesus and they leave the temple together. Mary understands her son is very special. She watches Jesus and remembers the day when the angel told her she was going to have a child.

8 Jesus teaching in the temple

Luke 2: 41-50

There is an uneven play of light in this painting, suggesting how the clever scripture scholars must have been puzzled and confused by hearing such a young boy teaching with such wisdom and certainty. Jesus is not only the source of the Light but also the source of knowledge.

'Why did you have to look for me? Didn't you know I had to be in my Father's house?'

Luke 2: 49

Questions for discussion

Have you ever been lost? How did it feel?

What did your family say when they found you?

Does your family worry about you? How do you know?

Do you ever take time to be alone in God's house?

What can you say to Jesus in your quiet times with him?

Everybody in your village has been talking about a very holy man. His name is John – John the Baptist. Every day, people gather by the River Jordan to listen to him preaching about God.

Make your way to the river bank. As you get closer you can hear John saying, "Repent, repent."

Watch the crowds queuing to be baptised. Go and join the queue. Right in front of you there is a man who is listening carefully to what John is saying. Watch as the man goes forward to be baptised. It's Jesus. He is about to be baptised.

Watch as Jesus walks into the water and moves towards John. They speak but you can't hear what they are saying. Jesus bows his head and disappears under the water. As he comes up from the water, the sky is filled with a bright light.

The crowds look to the sky and see a dove. Watch as it comes to rest above Jesus' head. A loud voice says, *"This is my son, the beloved. My favour rests on him."*

You whisper to yourself, "My son, the beloved."

Leave the river now and think for a moment. God is looking at you and saying, "This is my child the beloved."

9 Jesus baptised by John

Luke 3: 21-22; Mark 1: 9-11; Matthew 3: 13-17

The Holy Spirit appears and light takes on many colours, many gifts, great strength and dynamism, expressed by the swirling movement of the background. Jesus is anointed for his universal mission and endowed with power, confirmed in his calling by the Father's voice and the visible appearance of the Spirit. This is the Trinity manifested at the beginning of Jesus' great work of salvation.

'You are my own dear Son. I am pleased with you.'

Luke 3: 22

Questions for discussion

When were you baptised? What happened?

What promises were made when you were baptised?

How did God show he was happy that Jesus had been baptised?

How can the Holy Spirit help you in your life?

What has God done to show he loves you?

What can you do to show you return that love?

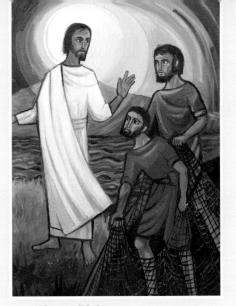

You are getting ready to go out fishing with your brother Simon. The nets need repairing. Sit down with your brother and start to repair the nets. As you work you think about your life. You are young.
Will you really be a fisherman for the rest of your life?

As you look along the shore you can see a figure making his way toward you.
It's Jesus. You've spent many days listening to his preaching. Jesus talks about really loving others – not just words, but real love.

Jesus is almost right by your boat. Perhaps he wants to speak to you? Perhaps he wants to go fishing?

Simon has stopped working. He is standing looking at Jesus. Nobody speaks. Then Jesus takes a step forward and says, *"Come follow me and I will make you fishers of men."* Watch as Simon drops the net and goes and follows Jesus.

Your heart is beating faster. Jesus is still standing there and now he is looking at you. Listen as he says, *"Come, follow me."*

Drop your net and follow Jesus. This really is what you have wanted to do all of your life. A little further along the shore James and John are mending their nets too. Watch as they both stop their work and feel the power of Jesus closely by. Jesus hasn't spoken yet but they know what he is going to say.

Watch as they turn to look at their father. Jesus smiles and says, *"Come, follow me."*

Together you walk away from the boats, away from the life you know. What will following Jesus really mean?

You turn and look at the footprints in the sand and wonder where Jesus will lead you.

10 Jesus calls his first disciples

Matthew 4: 18-22 Mark 1: 16-20

The same idea of light dominates this picture, the disciples being caught up in it and in the attraction of Jesus' personality. He calls them from darkness and immaturity (green) to the fullness of life and light (red) which for them will lead them to the consummation of martyrdom.

'Come with me and I will teach you to catch people.'

Mark 1: 17

Questions for discussion

Have you ever been asked to do something you really didn't want to do?

How did you make up your mind?

Do you ever find it hard to decide what to do? What happened?

What does it mean to be a follower of Jesus?

Where do you think Jesus is leading you?

How can you show other people that Jesus is important to you?

Imagine that you are Peter.
You are a very good friend of Jesus.
Think about the very first time you
saw Jesus. How did you feel?

Today you are travelling with Jesus
and the other disciples. You are
travelling to an area called Ceasarea
Philippi. You've been walking alongside Jesus for some time but he hasn't spoken
to you. You begin to wonder if something is the matter. Jesus looks very serious.

It's time to rest now and Jesus sits down. He asks you all a question.
'Who do people say the Son of Man is?'

Listen as the others answer – *'John the Baptist, Elijah, Jeremiah or one of the
prophets.'*

Jesus looks at you and says *'Who do you say that I am?'*
Your heart is beating very fast as you answer *'You are the Christ, the Son of the
Living God.'*

Jesus keeps looking straight at you and now his whole face is smiling. He puts his
hand on your shoulder and says *'Simon son of Jonah, you are a blessed man. My
father in heaven has taught you this.'*

You can't see or hear any of the other disciples. The only person you can see and
hear is Jesus. You feel very close to Jesus and ready to do anything that he will
ask. Jesus says 'You are Peter and on this rock I will build my community.' Jesus
knows that your name means rock and he smiles and puts his hand firmly on your
head. He is giving you a blessing. He is sharing his power because he wants you
to do a very important job.

Jesus tells you and the other disciples that you must not tell anybody that you
know and understand that he is God's Son.

You are ready now to do whatever Jesus asks. You know it won't be easy. You
begin to wonder how much longer Jesus will be with you.

11 Peter the Rock

Matthew 16: 13-20

The rock rises in the background, supporting Peter as he makes his profession of faith. Both Peter and the rock are suffused with the light flowing from Christ.

'You are a rock and on this rock foundation I will build my church.'

Matthew 16: 18

Questions for discussion

> Why do you think Jesus chose Simon Peter to be in charge of his Church?
>
> Why is Peter like a rock?
>
> Do you ever talk about Jesus? Who do you talk to?
>
> Who is in charge of God's church today?
>
> What can you do to help build God's Church?

Teaching guide

At McCrimmons we recognise that planning with today's popular R.E. programmes is often a difficult and time-consuming task. This brief guide has been written to help you make the most of these posters without having to spend a long time looking for resources and information.

Here I Am & Walk With Me

The table on the opposite page is cross-referenced to the themes in the *Here I Am* and *Walk With Me* catechetical programmes. If you are short of time, we hope the table might provide a quick solution for teachers and catechists who are under pressure of work. The bold headings at the top refer to the stages of the R.E. programmes.

General themes

We have also included some general themes (under the *Others* heading) that may help you integrate the posters into other R.E. programmes. You may also want to adapt the posters and booklet material to suit the individual needs of your own school or parish.

Developing the material

If you have the opportunity, we recommend that you spend more time developing your own thematic index that suits the needs of your own unique situation. All the best R.E. teaching comes when the teacher or catechist has really thought about the needs of the children concerned and planned well with those needs in mind. We hope this table will be a useful starting point.

JESUS, OUR LIGHT (1)	N/R	ONE	TWO	THREE	FOUR
John the Baptist *Luke 1:5-25*				Preparations	Visitors
The Annunciation *Luke 1:26-38*			Birthdays, Visitors	Invitations, Birthdays Preparations	Birthdays
The Visitation *Luke 1:39-56*			Visitors	Babies, Preparations Visitors	Birthdays
The Nativity *Luke 2:4-7*	Birthdays, Preparations Gifts, Visitors	Birthdays, Visitors Preparations, Gifts	Babies, Birthdays Preparations, Gifts	Birthdays, Preparations Gifts	Birthdays
The Visit of the Shepherds *Luke 2:7-20*	Birthdays, Preparations Gifts, Visitors	Preparations, Gifts Visitors	Birthdays, Gifts		Gifts
The Visit of the Magi *Matthew 2:1-12*	Birthdays, Preparations Gifts, Visitors	Preparations, Gifts Visitors	Birthdays, Preparations Gifts	Birthdays, Gifts	Gifts
The Flight into Egypt *Matthew 2:13-18*					
The Presentation *Luke 2:22-38*	Special People Celebrations	Special People Celebrations	Special People, Books Celebrations	Celebrations	Special People
The Finding in the Temple *Luke 2:41-50*	Special People	Special People		Journeys	
The Baptism of Jesus *Mark 1:9-11*					
The Calling of the the Disciples *Mark 1:16-20*				Special People	Invitations
Jesus Chooses Peter *Matthew 4:18-20 / 16:13-20*				Special People	Special People

Jesus, Our Life poster series

THE BENEDICTINE NUNS OF TURVEY ABBEY

Part 2 **Jesus, Our Way**

The next step in this exciting and highly acclaimed poster series shows us the way Jesus leads us – through suffering and death to the glory of the Resurrection and the coming of the Holy Spirit. Twelve posters suitable for use at Lent & Easter.

12 Full colour laminated posters / Size: A2 / Ref: LOC2P

Part 3 **Jesus, Our Hope**

In this set of posters based on the Life of Jesus, we follow the Ministry of Our lord in the colourful depictions of his miracles, parables and others events, which build our faith and lead us in hope.

12 Full colour laminated posters / Size: A2 / Ref: LOC3P

God's Promise

A set of posters illustrating the power of the Old Testament. Starting at Genesis with a vibrant depiction of God's Creation and on to God's Blessing to Abraham and his people. Exodus follows with Moses receiving the Ten Commandments and then to Joshua and the story of the Promised Land. This colourful poster set carries on to illustrate some more of the fascinating stories from Scripture.

12 Full colour laminated posters / Size: A2 / Ref: POT1

1 **Breath of the Spirit**
2 **Spirit Alive**

SISTER SHEILA GOSNEY

Two striking sets of posters. The first is an ideal resource for confirmation programmes, the second expresses the external imagery of the Holy Spirit – Fire, Wind and Water the Dove – and other symbols of the life of the Christian church. Each poster, with the help of an accompanying booklet, may be used to explore the messages of the Scriptures.

Breath of the Spirit
8 Full colour laminated posters and guide booklet / Size: A2 / Ref: MPCP1
Spirit Alive
8 Full colour laminated posters and guide booklet / Size: A2 / Ref: MPSA

The Footsteps of Christ

THE BENEDICTINE NUNS OF TURVEY ABBEY

This popular set has been created from 16 glorious oil paintings by the Benedictine Nuns of Turvey Abbey. Suitable for Lent & Easter, the posters follow Christ along the journey of the Cross from Peter's denial to the entombment and ending with the joy and hope of the resurrection.

16 Full colour laminated posters (includes FREE book) / Size: A2 / Ref: FOCP